2015 GREATEST POP & MOVIE HITS

ARRANGED BY
CAROL MATZ

CONTENTS

Alfred

Produced by
Alfred Music
P.O. Box 10003
Van Nuys, CA 91410-0003
alfred.com

Printed in USA.

ISBN-10: 1-4706-2324-2
ISBN-13: 978-1-4706-2324-1

Cover Photo: © Shutterstock.com / Vladitto

AIN'T IT FUN

Words and Music by
Hayley Williams and Taylor York
Arr. Carol Matz

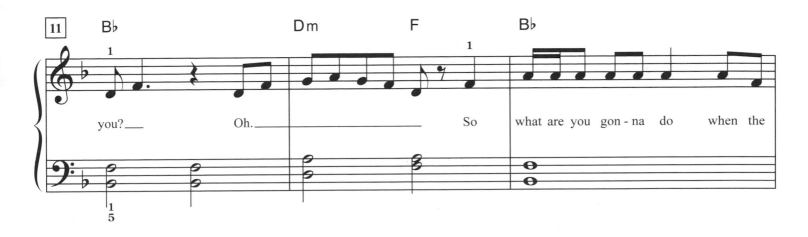

Chorus:

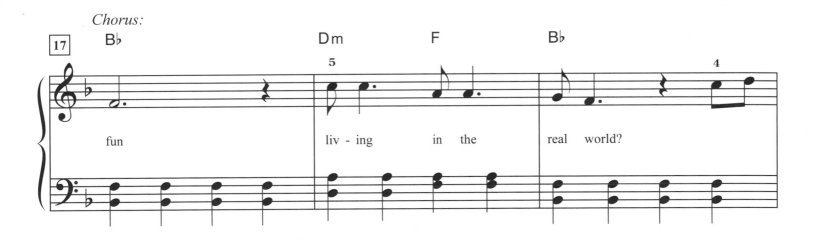

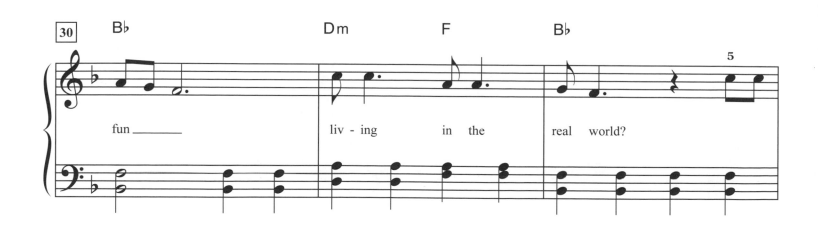

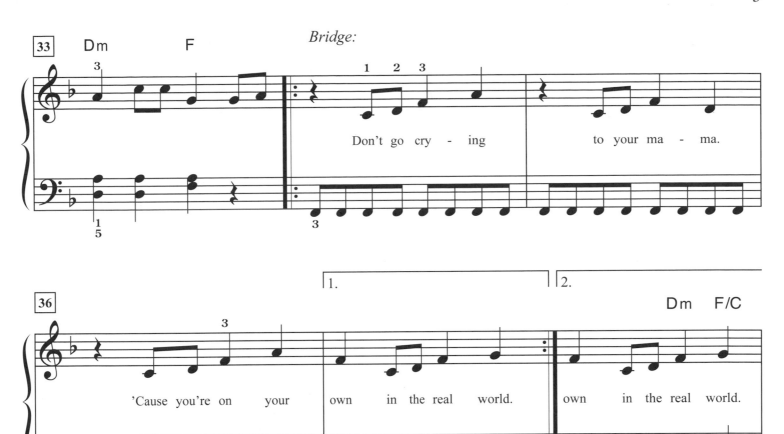

Bridge:

Don't go cry - ing to your ma - ma.

'Cause you're on your own in the real world. own in the real world.

Don't go cry - ing to your ma - ma. 'Cause you're on your

own in the real world. Don't go cry - ing to your ma - ma.

Verse 2:
Where you're from, you might be the one who's running things.
Well, you can ring anybody's bell and get what you want.
You see, it's easy to ignore trouble when you're living in a bubble.
So what are you gonna do when the world don't orbit around you? Oh.
So what are you gonna do when nobody wants to fool with you?

ALL ABOUT THAT BASS

Words and Music by
Meghan Trainor and Kevin Kadish
Arr. Carol Matz

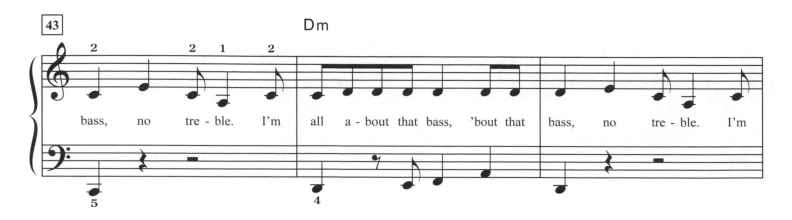

Verse 2:
I'm bringing booty back.
Go ahead and tell them skinny ****** that.
No, I'm just playing. I know you think you're fat,
But I'm here to tell you, ev'ry inch of you is perfect
From the bottom to the top.

ALONE YET NOT ALONE

Music by Bruce Broughton
Lyrics by Dennis Spiegel
Arr. Carol Matz

BELIEVER

Words and Music by Zachary Barnett,
James Adam Shelley, Matthew Sanchez,
David Rublin, Shep Goodman and Aaron Accetta
Arr. Carol Matz

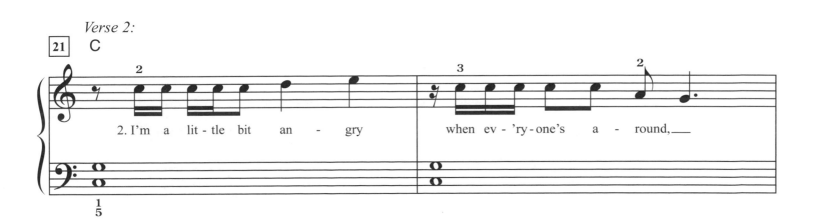

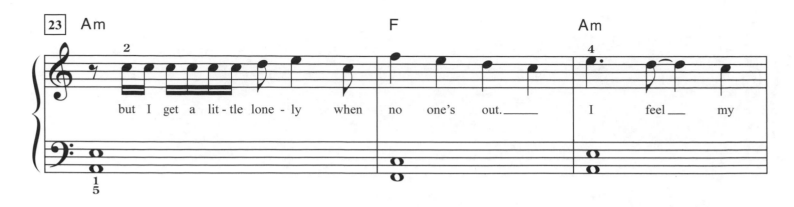

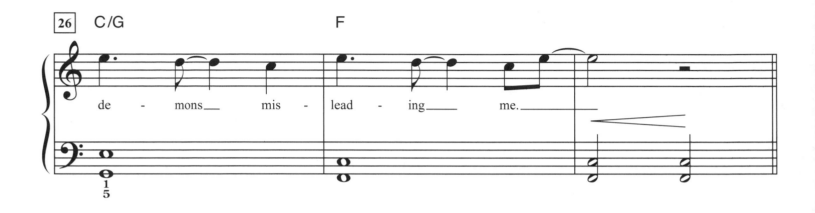

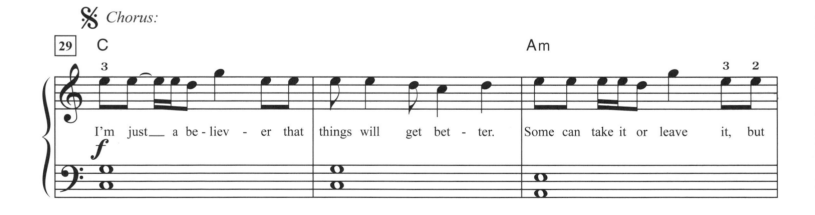

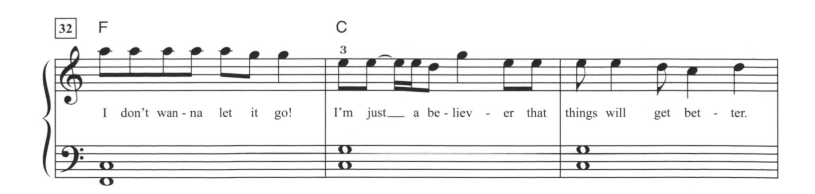

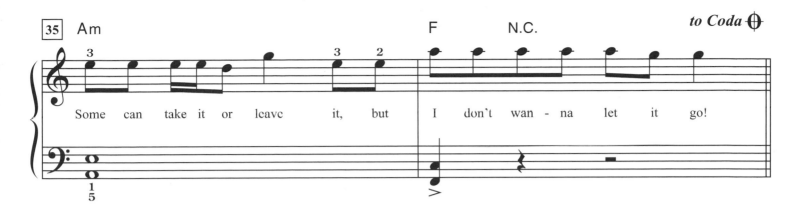

Verse 3:

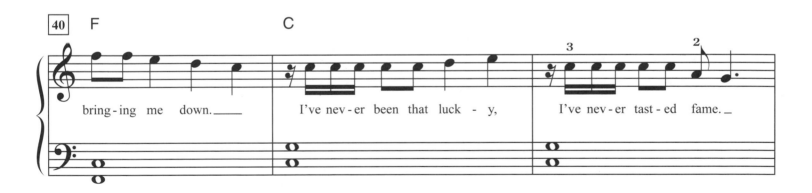

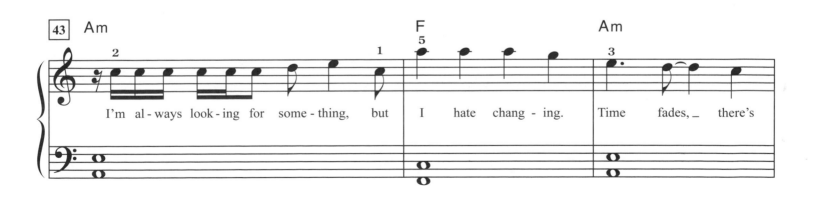

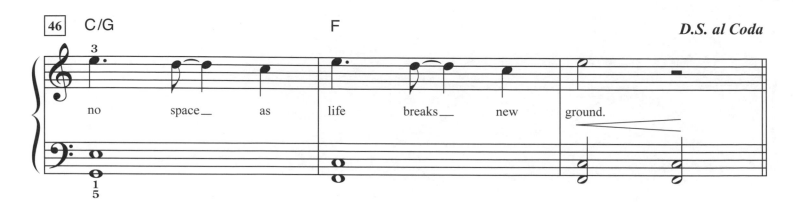

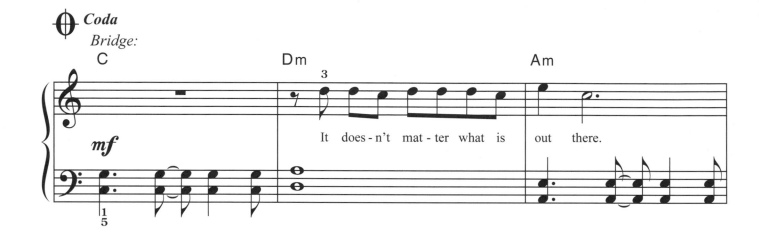

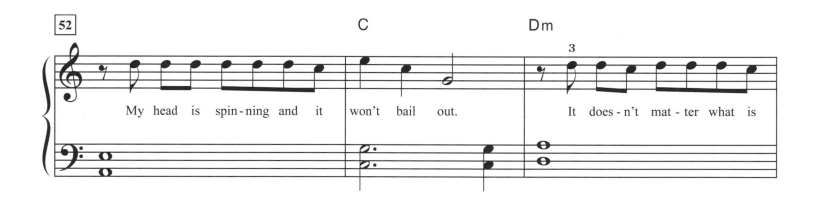

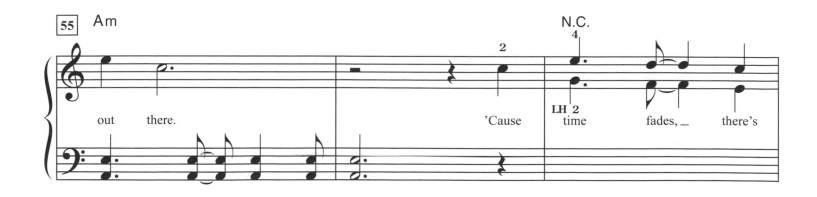

no space___ as | life breaks___ new | ground._____

Chorus:
Play 3 times

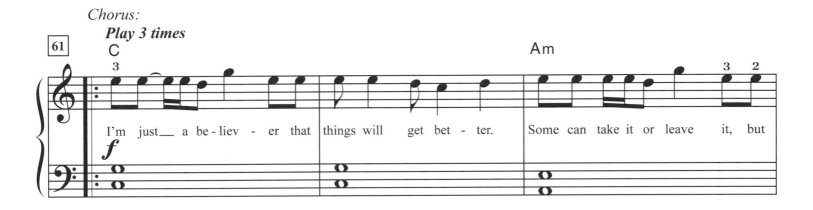

I'm just___ a be - liev - er that | things will get bet - ter. | Some can take it or leave it, but

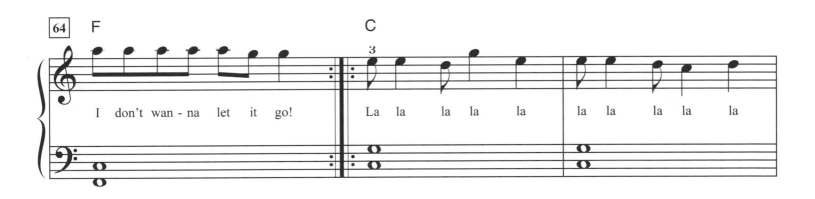

I don't wan - na let it go! | La la la la la | la la la la la

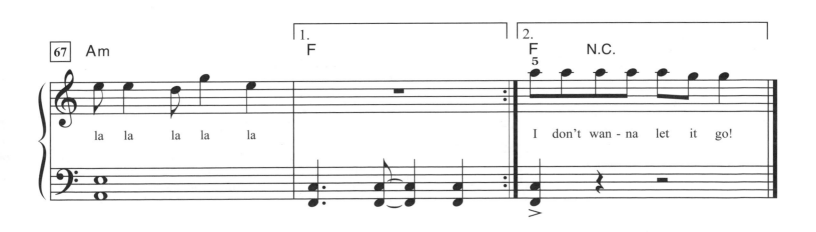

la la la la la | | I don't wan - na let it go!

BEST DAY OF MY LIFE

Words and Music by Zachary Barnett,
James Adam Shelley, Matthew Sanchez,
David Rublin, Shep Goodman and Aaron Accetta
Arr. Carol Matz

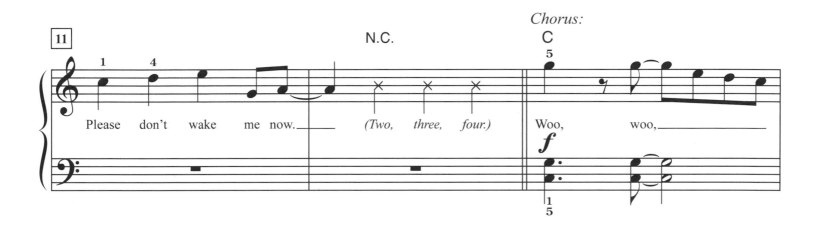

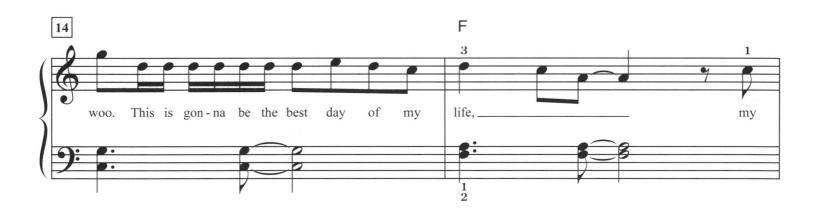

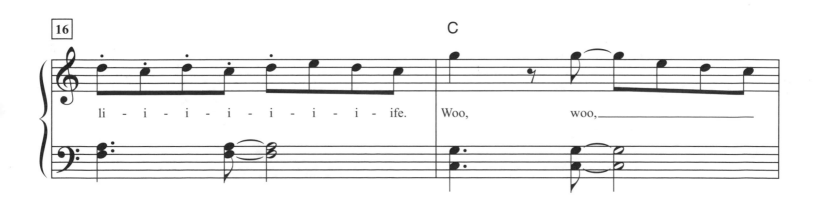

woo. This is gon-na be the best day of my life,_____ my

li - i - i - i - i - i - i - ife. Woo, woo,_____ woo.

Verse 2:

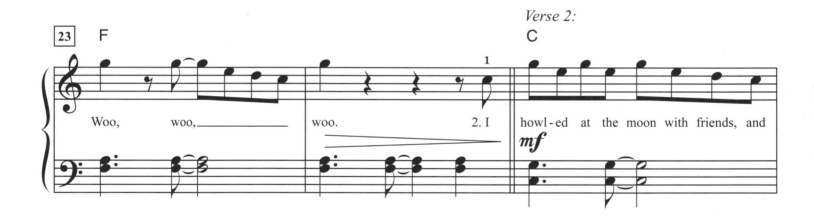

Woo, woo,_____ woo. 2. I howl-ed at the moon with friends, and

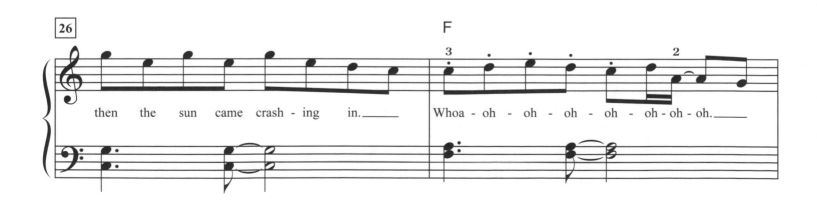

then the sun came crash - ing in._____ Whoa - oh - oh - oh - oh - oh - oh - oh.____

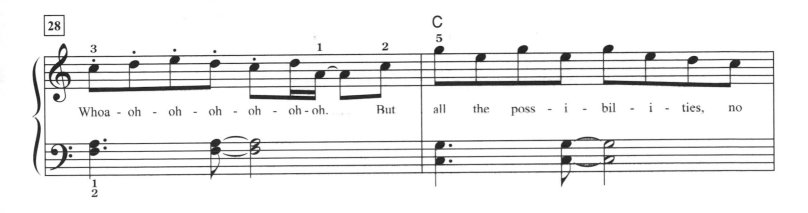

Whoa - oh - oh - oh - oh - oh - oh. But all the poss - i - bil - i - ties, no

lim - its, just e - piph - an - ies._____ Whoa - oh - oh - oh - oh - oh - oh - oh._____

Whoa - oh - oh - oh - oh - oh - oh._____ I'm nev - er gon - na look back, whoa,_____ I'm

nev - er gon - na give it up, no._____ Just don't wake me now._____

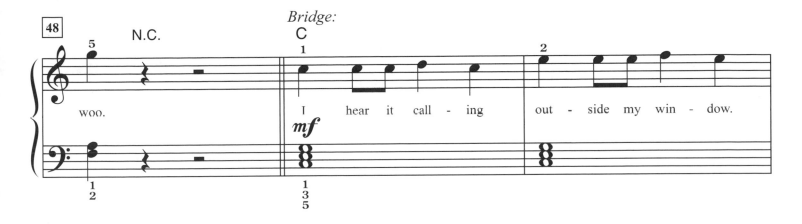

woo.

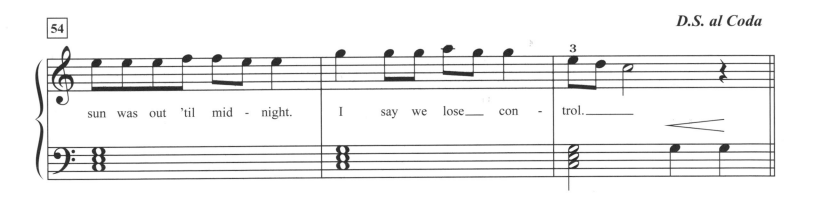

BEYOND THE FOREST

(from *The Hobbit: The Desolation of Smaug*)

Music by Howard Shore
Lyrics by Philippa Boyens
Arr. Carol Matz

ped. simile

CLOUDS

Words and Music by Zach Sobiech
Arr. Carol Matz

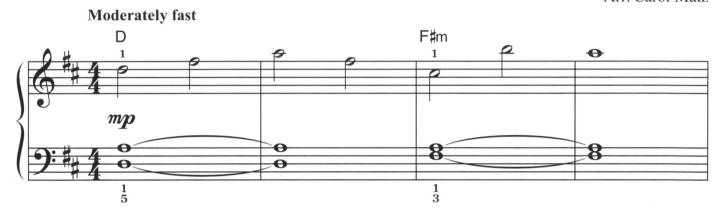

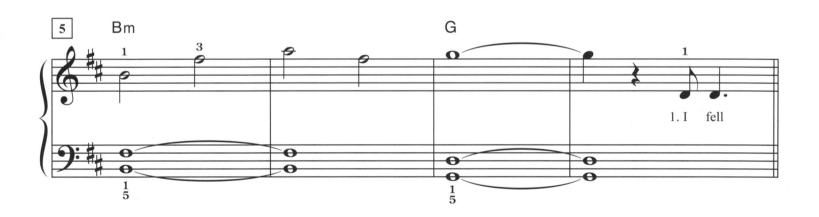

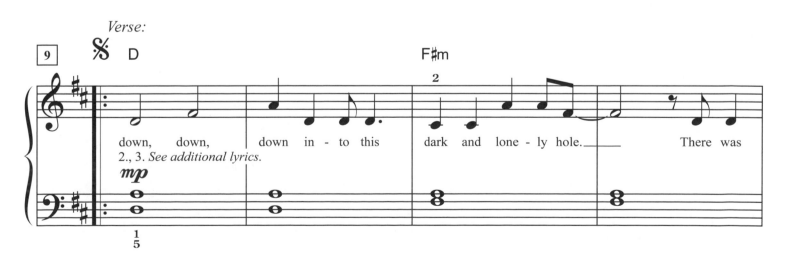

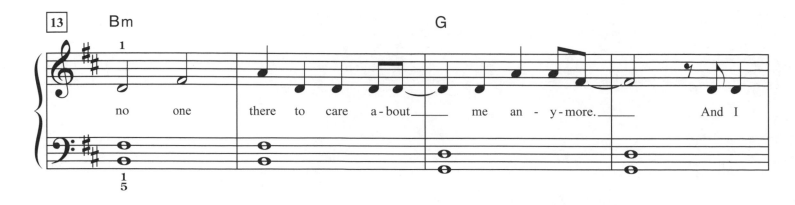

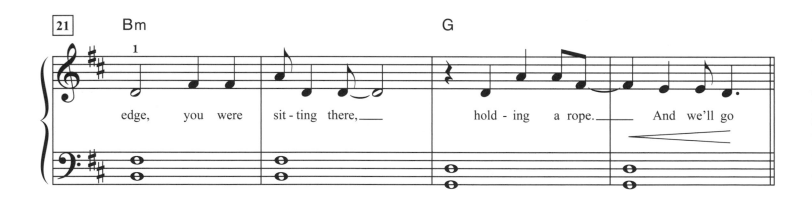

Chorus:

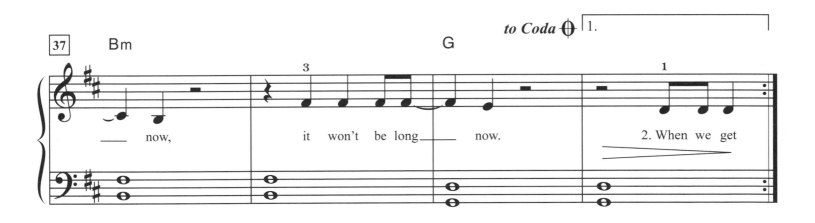

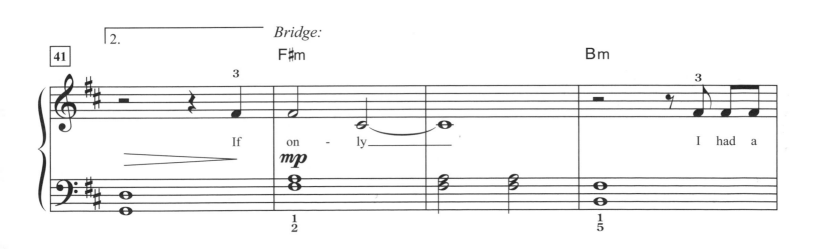

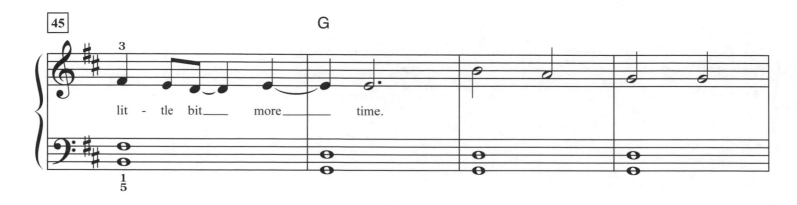

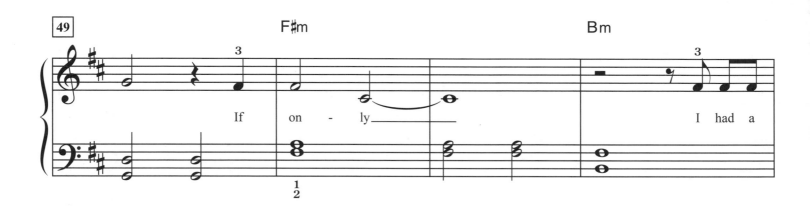

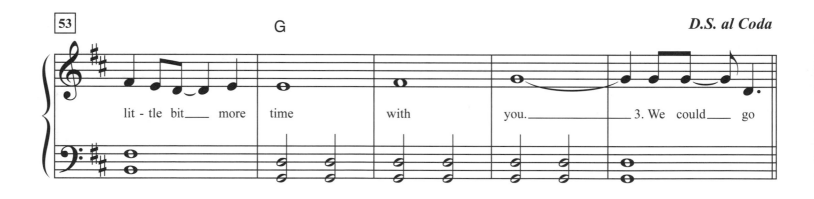

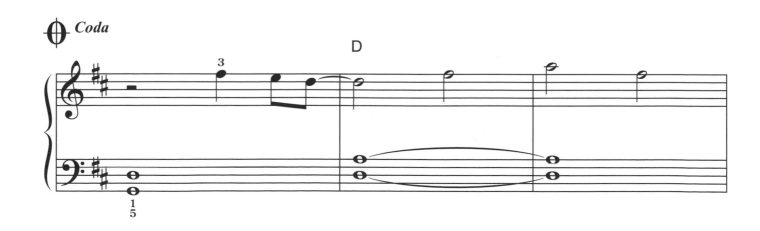

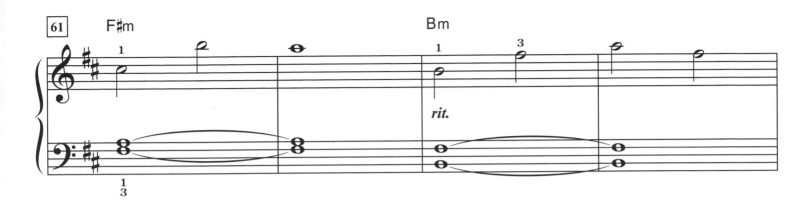

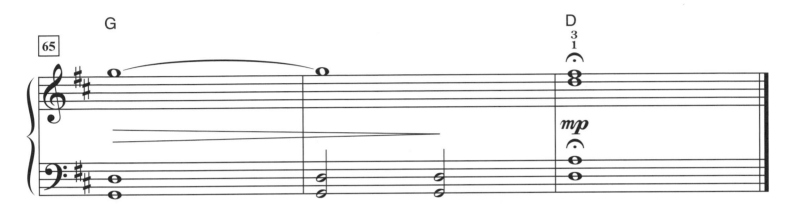

Verse 2:
When we get back on land,
Well, I'll never get my chance,
Be ready to live and it'll be
Ripped right out of my hands.
And maybe some day
We'll take a little ride,
We'll go up, up, up
And everything will be just fine.
(To Chorus:)

Verse 3:
We could go up, up, up,
Up and take that little ride,
We'll sit there holding hands
And everything would be just right.
And maybe someday
I'll see you again,
We'll float up in the clouds
And we'll never see the end.
(To Chorus:)

CAN YOU HEAR YOUR HEART?

(from *Winter's Tale*)

Music by Hans Zimmer,
Ann Marie Calhoun and Rupert Gregson-Williams
Arr. Carol Matz

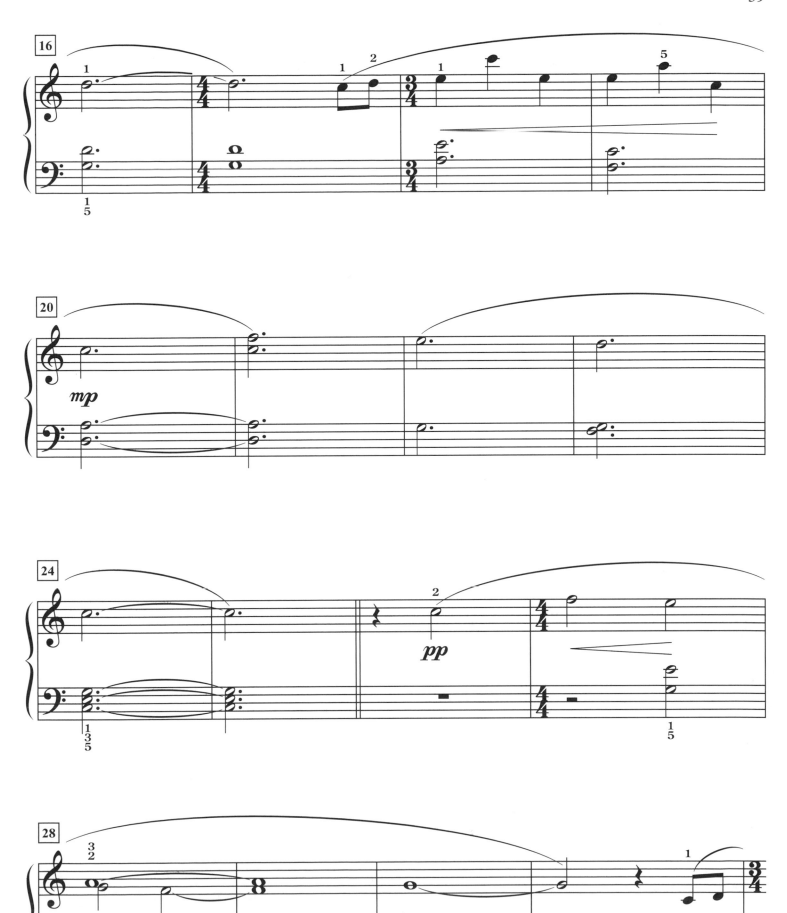

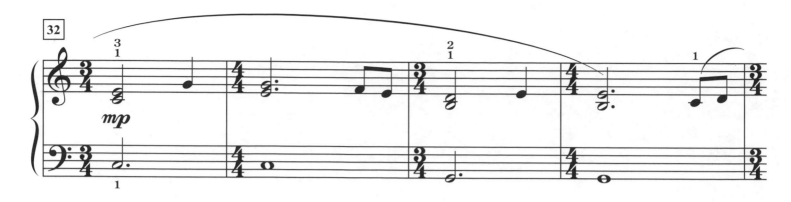

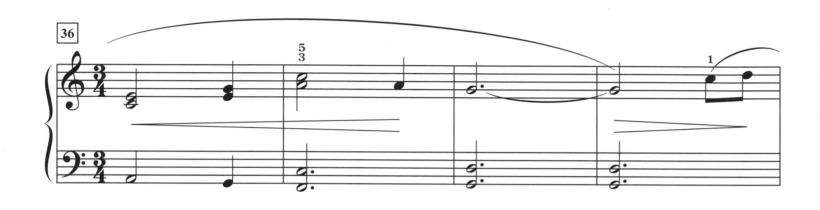

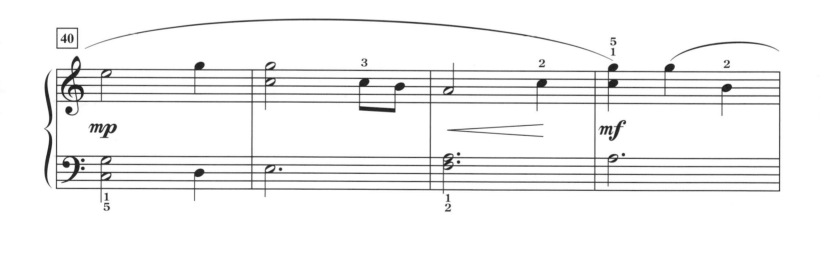

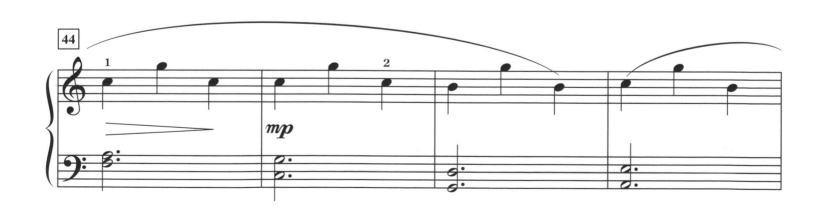

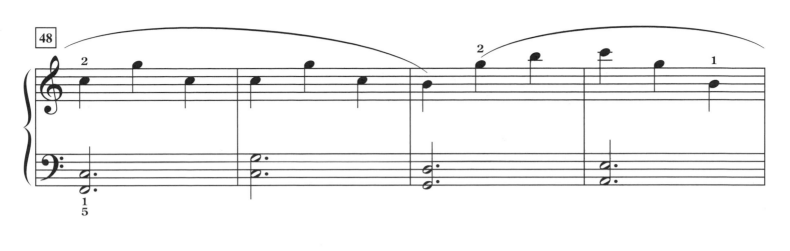

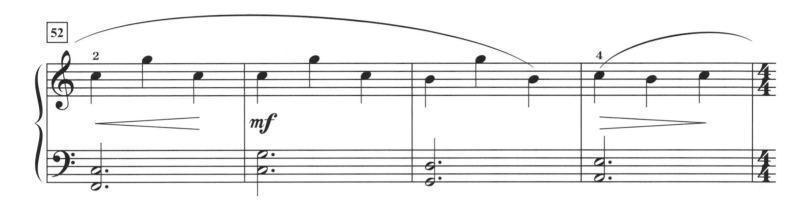

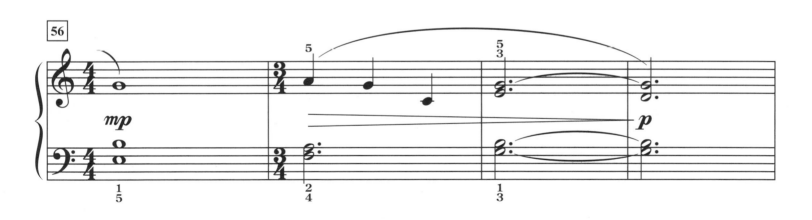

COMING UP ROSES

Words and Music by
Glen Hansard and Danielle Brisebois
Arr. Carol Matz

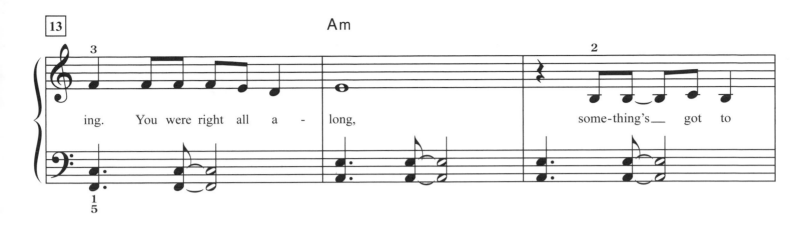

Chorus:

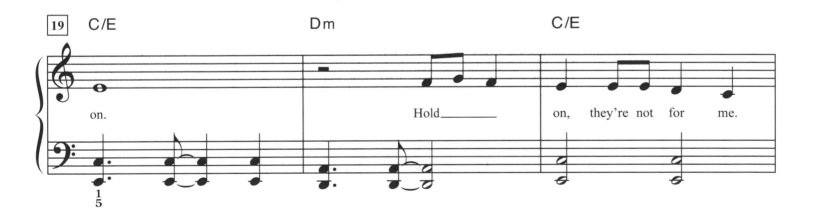

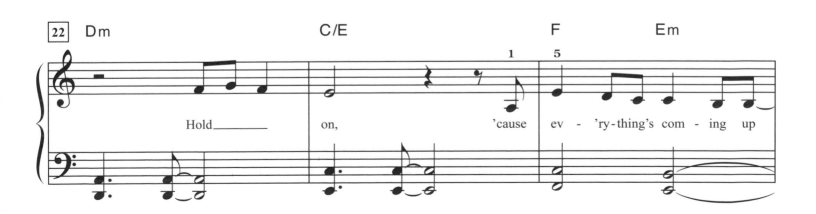

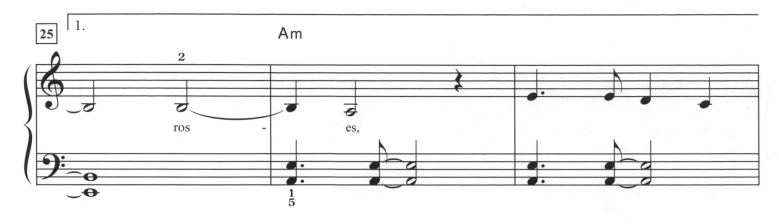

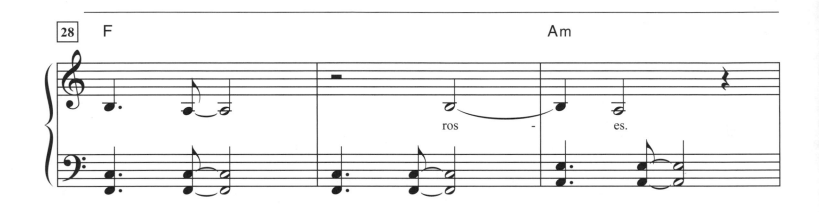

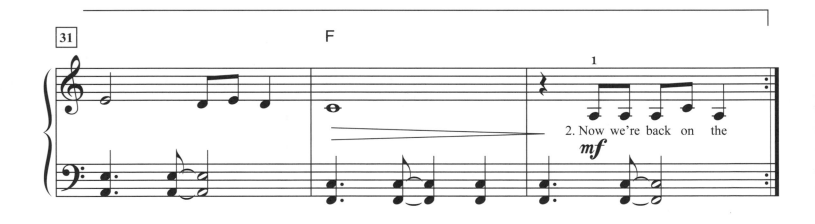

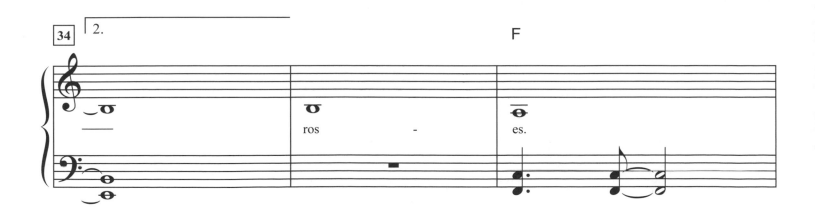

Chorus:

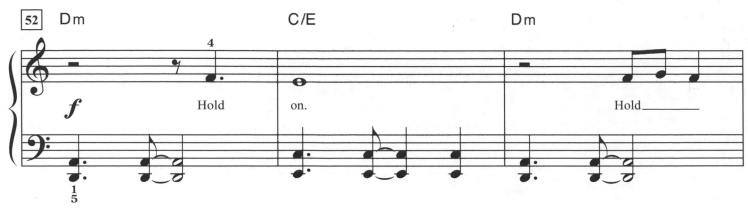

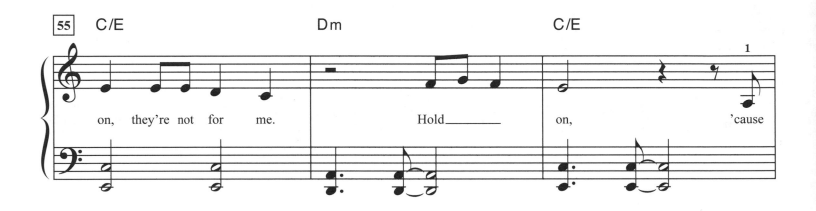

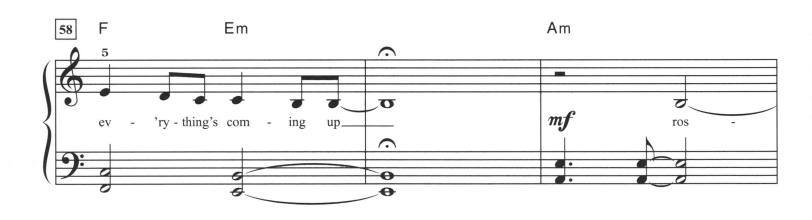

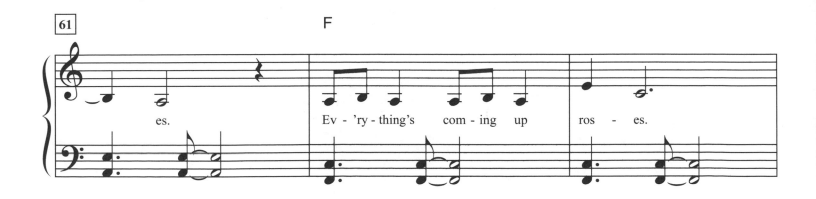

Verse 2:
Now we're back on the street,
Found a song that's worth singing.
The blur that knows a defeat
While your victory bell's ringing.
My whole life's turned around,
For this thing you keep chasing.
You were right all along,
But it's me who's got to change.
(To Chorus:)

COOL KIDS

Words and Music by Graham Sierota,
Jamie Sierota, Noah Sierota, Sydney Sierota,
Jeffery David Sierota and Jesiah Dzwonek
Arr. Carol Matz

Moderately

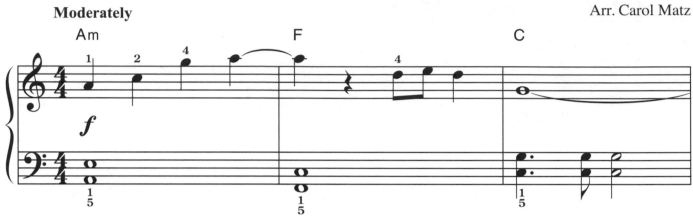

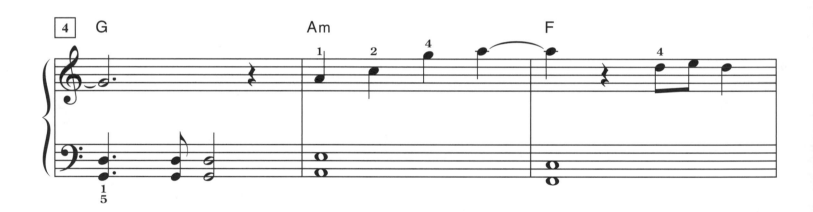

Verse:

1. She sees them walk-ing in a straight line;
2. *See additional lyrics.*

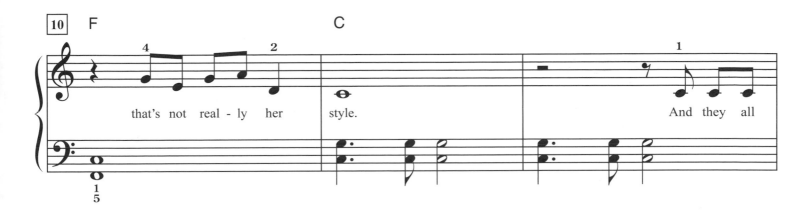

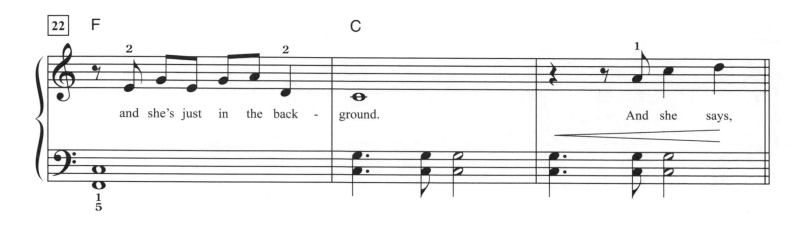

Chorus:

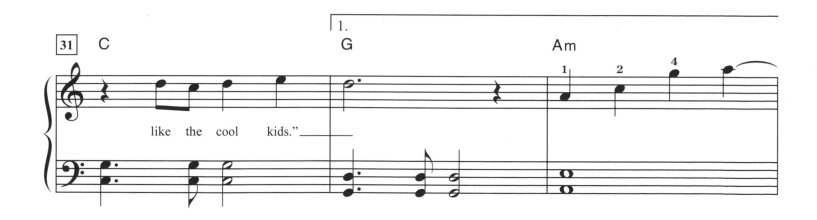

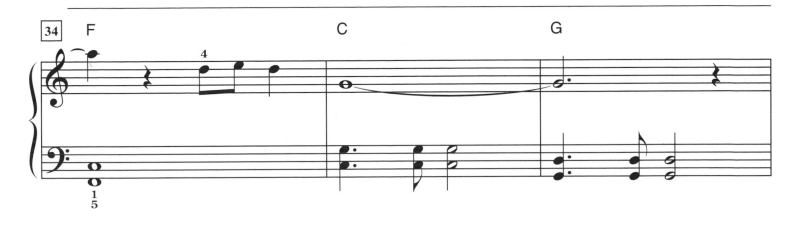

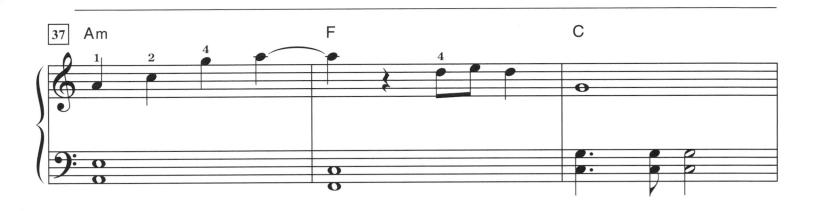

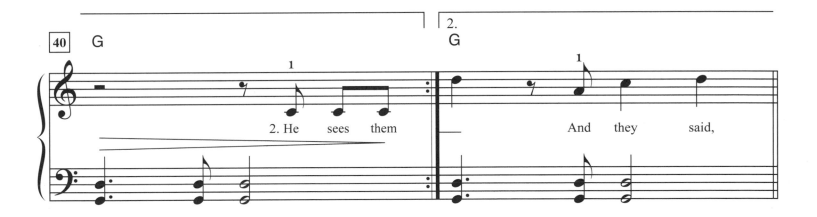

Chorus:

52

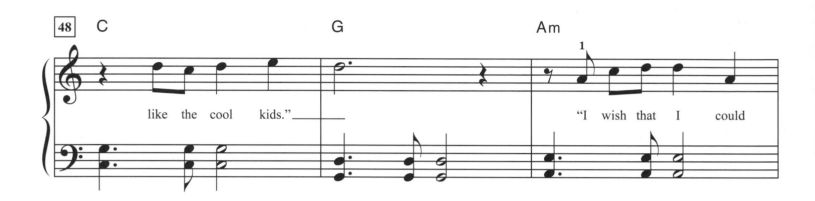

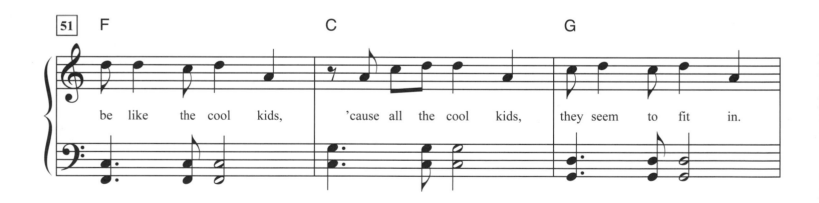

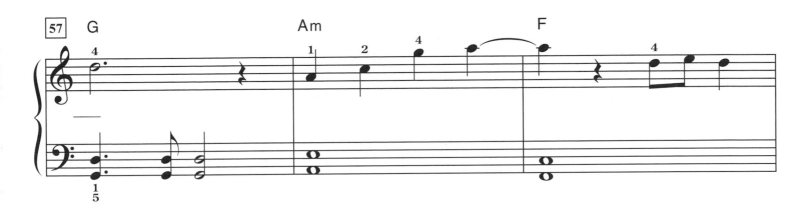

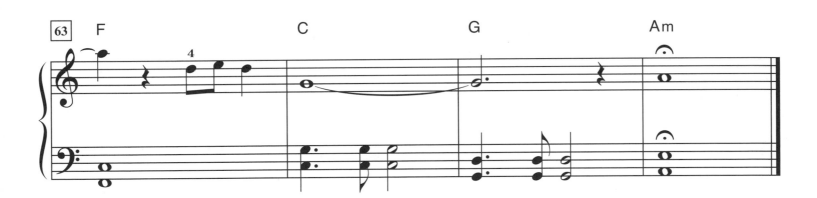

Verse 2:
He sees them talking with a big smile,
But they haven't got a clue.
Yeah, they're living the good life;
Can't see what he is going through.
They're driving fast cars,
But they don't know where they're going;
In the fast lane, living life without knowing.
And he says,
(To Chorus:)

DOIN' WHAT SHE LIKES

Words and Music by
Wade Kirby and Phil O'Donnell
Arr. Carol Matz

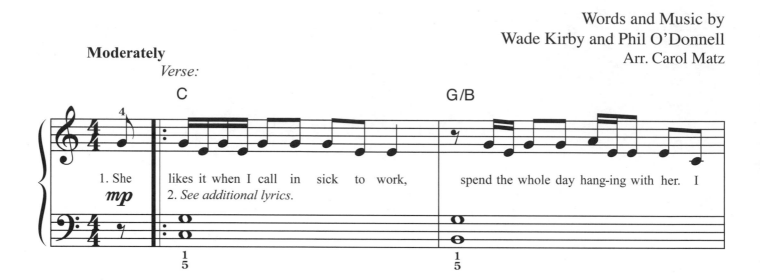

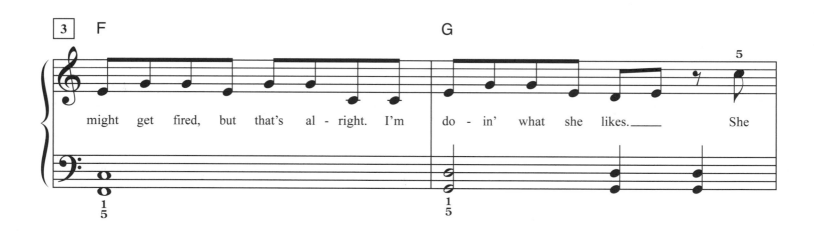

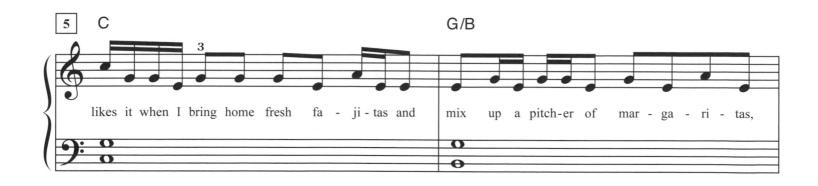

56

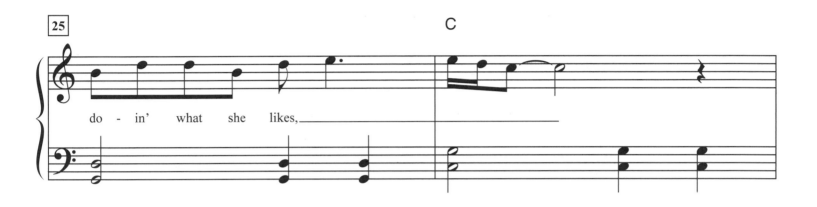

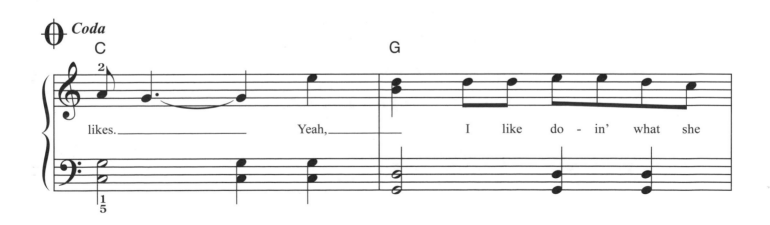

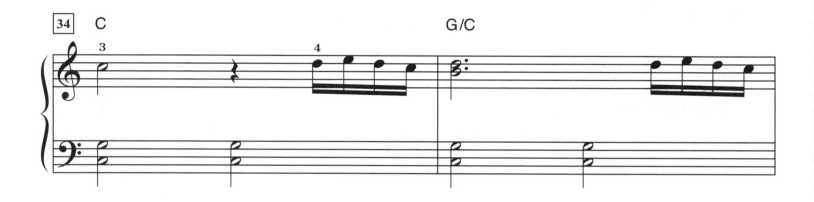

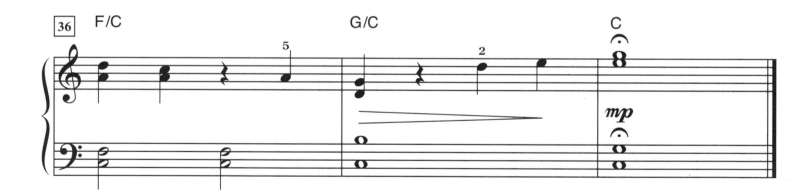

Verse 2:
She likes it when I get past second gear,
Sees gravel flying in the rearview mirror.
Sometimes I'm pushin' ninety-five
Doin' what she likes.
And she likes it when I find a road that's dark.
Can we pull off somewhere and park?
Turn the radio on and turn off the lights;
Keep doin' what she likes.
(To Chorus:)

EVERYTHING IS AWESOME

(Awesome Remixxx!!!) (from *The Lego Movie*)

Music by Shawn Patterson
Lyrics by Shawn Patterson, Andy Samberg,
Akiva Schaffer, Jorma Taccone,
Joshua Bartholomew and Lisa Harriton

Arr. Carol Matz

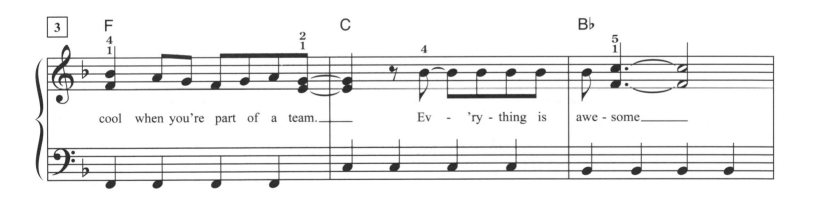

Bridge:

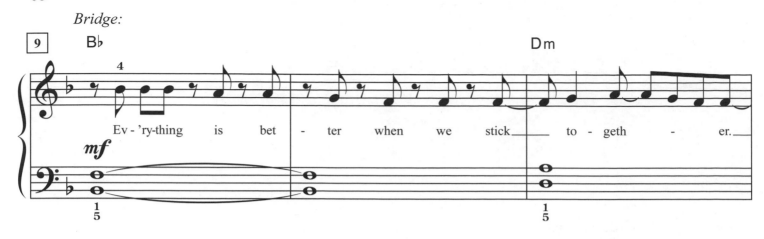

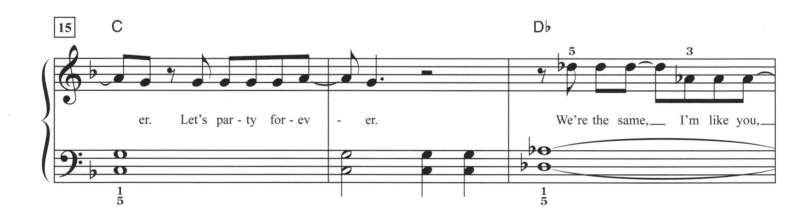

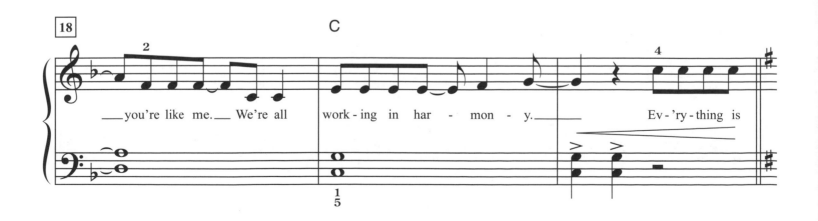

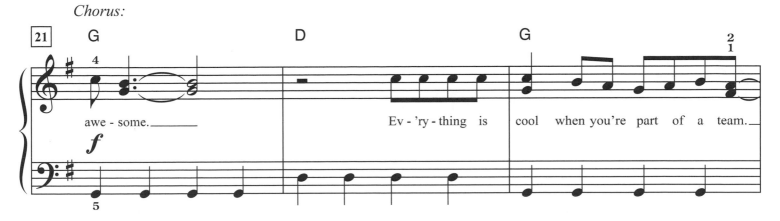

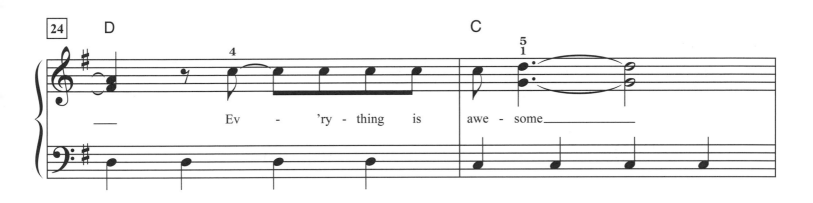

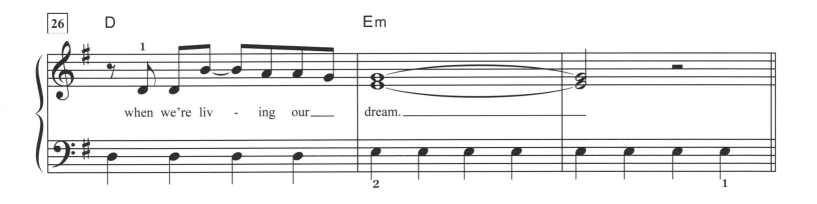

to Coda ⊕

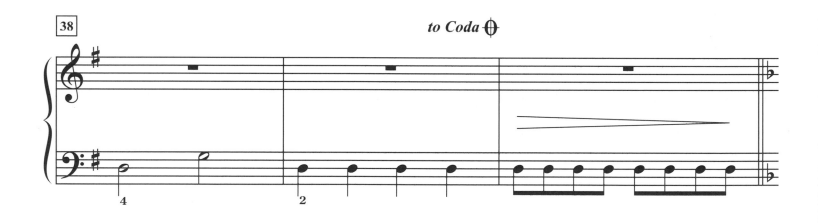

Bridge:

Bb   Dm

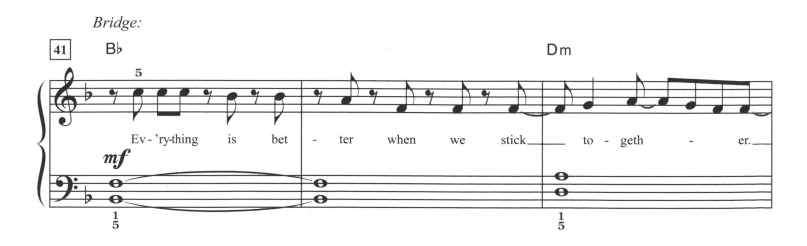

Ev - 'ry-thing is bet - ter when we stick____ to - geth - er.____

mf

Side by side, you and I gon - na win____ for - ev -

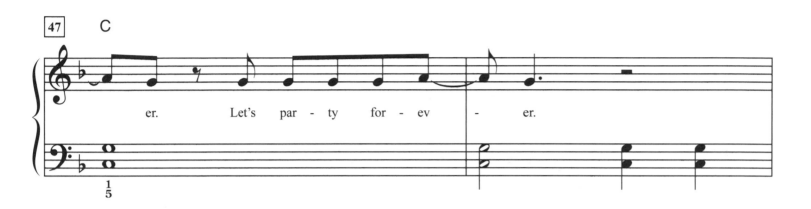

er. Let's par - ty for - ev - er.

We're the same,____ I'm like you,____ you're like me.____ We're all

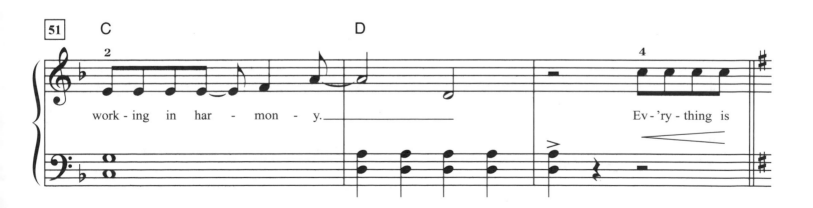

work - ing in har - mon - y.____ Ev - 'ry - thing is

64

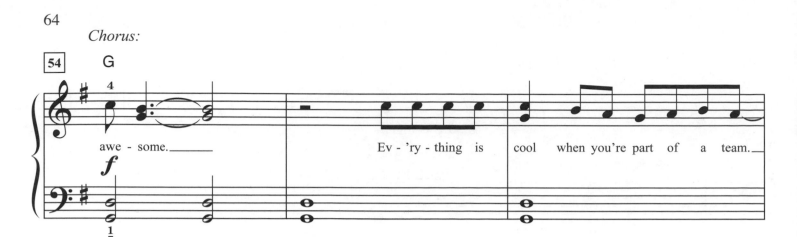

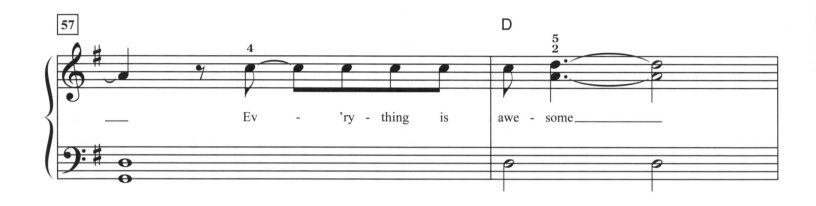

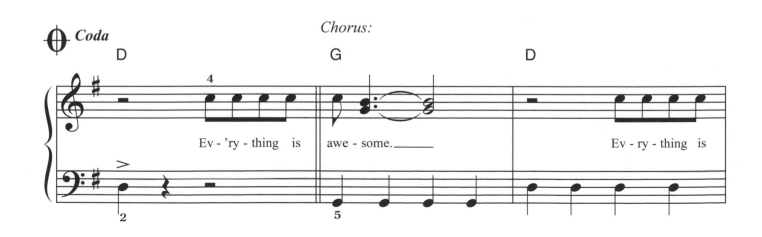

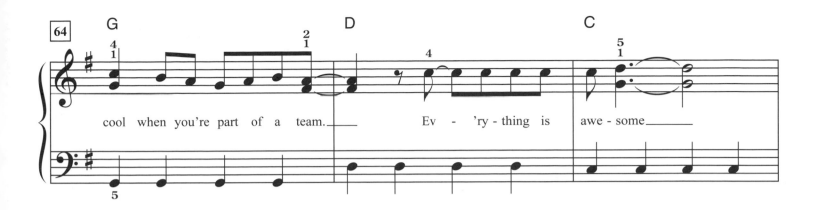

cool when you're part of a team.____ Ev - 'ry - thing is awe - some____

when we're liv - ing our____ dream.

Rap 1:

Have you heard the news? Everyone's talkin'.
Life is good cause everything's awesome.
Lost my job, there's a new opportunity,
More free time for my awesome community.
I feel more awesome than an awesome possum,
Dip my body in chocolate frostin'.
Three years later wash off the frostin'.
Smellin' like a blossom, everything is awesome.
Stepped in mud, got new brown shoes.
It's awesome to win and it's awesome to lose.
(To Bridge:)

Rap 2:

Blue skies, bouncy springs,
We just named two awesome things.
A Nobel Prize, a piece of string.
You know what's awesome? EVERYTHING!
Dogs with fleas,
Allergies,
A book of Greek antiquities,
Brand new pants, a very old vest,
Awesome items are the best.
Trees, frogs, clogs, they're awesome!
Rocks, clocks and socks, they're awesome!
Figs and jigs and twigs, that's awesome!
Everything you see or think or say is awesome!
(To Chorus:)

GRAVITY

Composed by Steven Price
Arr. Carol Matz

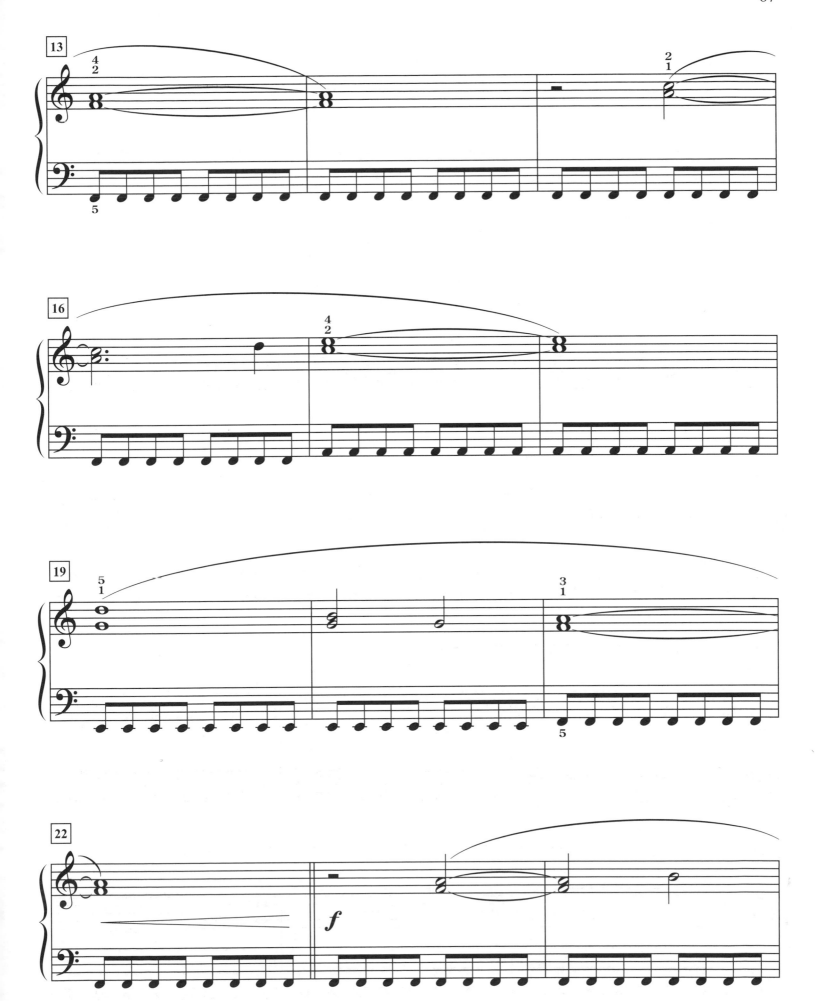

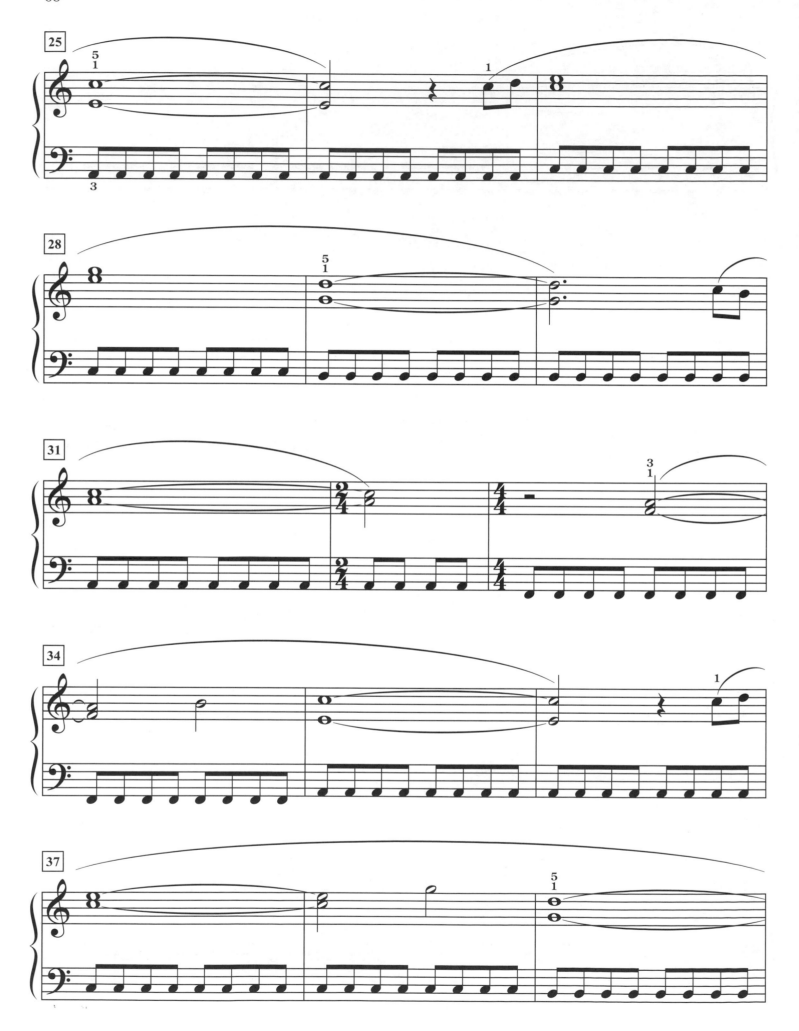

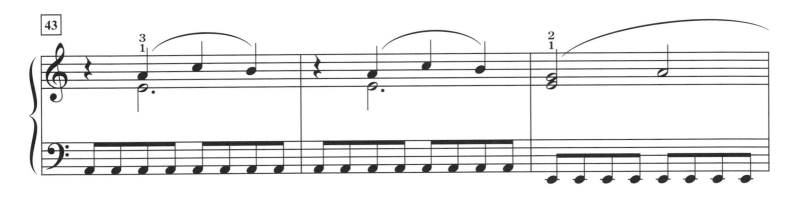

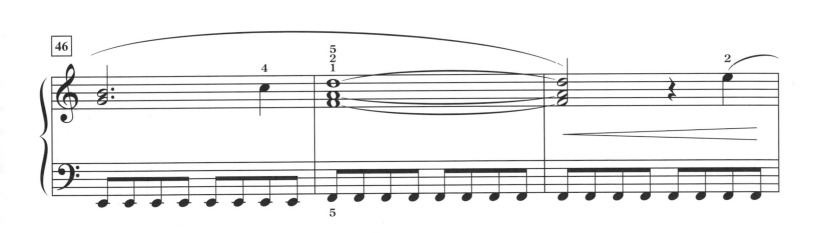

I SEE FIRE

(from *The Hobbit: The Desolation of Smaug*)

Words and Music by Ed Sheeran
Arr. Carol Matz

72

74

ROAR

Words and Music by Katy Perry, Bonnie McKee,
Max Martin, Lukasz Gottwald and Henry Walter
Arr. Carol Matz

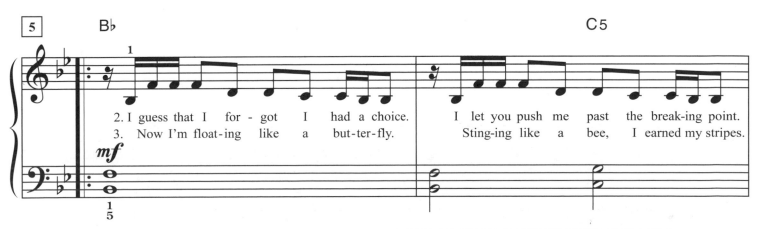

Pre-Chorus:

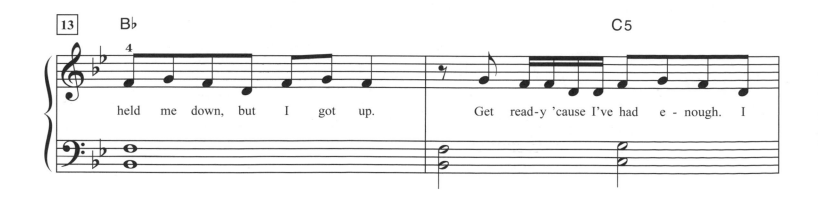

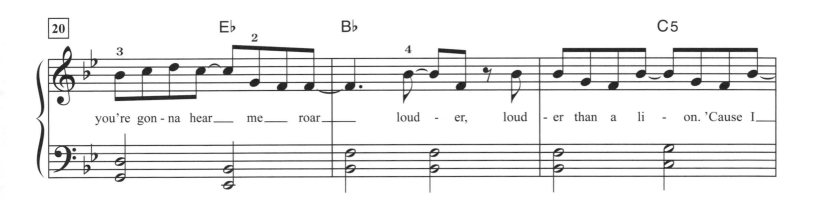

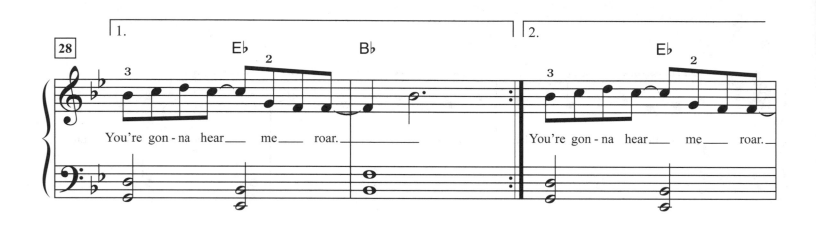

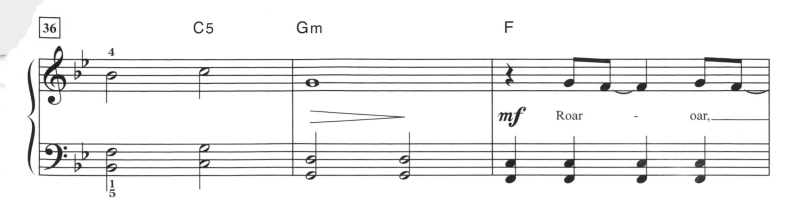

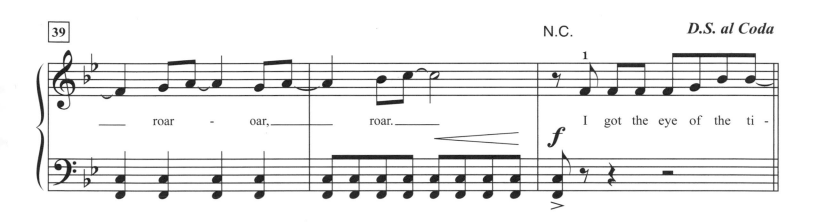